The Paris Commune

An account of the dramatic days between March and May 1871, when a working-class government overthrew the established order and set up a Commune in Paris. This book tells the fascinating story of the day-to-day existence of the Commune under siege conditions, its brief moment of glory, and its bloody defeat. But it was defeat only in a short-term sense. The ideas and reforms proposed by the Communards had a profound effect on nineteenth and twentieth-century socialist thinking, and the issues which were debated with such intensity by ordinary people of the time are ones which still confront us today.

THE INTERNATIONALE

Arise! ye starvelings from your slumbers,
   Arise ye criminals of want,
For reason in revolt now thunders,
   And at last ends the age of cant.
Now away with all superstitions,
   Servile masses, arise! arise!
We'll change forthwith the old conditions,
   And spurn the dust to win the prize.

Chorus
   Then comrades, come rally,
      The last fight let us face,
   L'Internationale,
      Unites the human race.

This famous socialist song
was written by Communard
Eugène Pottier.

The
Paris
Commune

MARY KENNEDY

Collins

For Iain for later.

Several friends lived through and helped in the making of this book. To them I owe great thanks; in particular to Gino Avanzi, Emma Cullinan, Christopher Johnson, Peter Martin, Nancy Fortescue of the University of Sussex, Eric Willats and Arthur Brooks of the Central Reference Library, Islington, London.

William Collins Sons & Co Ltd
London · Glasgow · Sydney · Auckland
Toronto · Johannesburg

First published 1979
Text © Mary Kennedy 1979
ISBN 0 00 195632 9

Made and printed in Great Britain by
William Collins Sons & Co Ltd Glasgow

Contents

Diary of Events 1870-71

19 July **1870**	France declares war on Prussia.
4 September	News of the French defeat and surrender of the Emperor at Sedan reach population of Paris. The Republic proclaimed.
18 September	Prussians begin the siege of Paris.
31 October	Riots in Paris after French surrender at Metz.
5 January **1871**	Prussians begin bombardment of Paris.
18 January	Proclamation of the German Empire at Versailles.
28 January	Armistice between France and Germany signed. End of siege.
8 February	General elections throughout France for the National Assembly.
15 February	Pay of the National Guards cancelled, unless proof of need.
17 February	Thiers elected leader of the government by the National Assembly.
26-28 February	Rebellious National Guards seize over 200 cannon and transport them to Montmartre.
1 March	Victorious entry of the German army into Paris.
15 March	Central Committee of the National Guard elected.
18 March	Government attempt to recapture the cannon at Montmartre sparks off uprising by Parisians. Government flee to Versailles.
19 March	National Guard Central Committee announce elections for the Commune.
22 March to 4 April	Communes in Lyons, Toulouse, St-Etienne, Narbonne and Marseilles suppressed.
26 March	Elections in Paris for the Commune.
28 March	The newly-elected members of the Commune take power.
29 March	The Commune issues its first decrees.
30 March	Civil war between the Paris Commune and the government at Versailles.

4 April	Communard forces defeated by government troops and many Communard prisoners shot on the battlefield. Archbishop of Paris arrested as a hostage of the Commune.
6 April	Public burning of the guillotine in the Place Voltaire.
11 April	Formation of the Women's Union for the Defence of Paris and Aid to the Wounded.
14 April	First meeting of the Artists' Federation headed by the painter, Courbet.
16 April	Commune declares policy on abandoned workshops, and agrees a 3 year period to repay all debts.
19 April	The Commune's declaration to the French people outlining aims and programme.
20 April	Night work for bakers prohibited.
1 May	Committee of Public Safety formed. Versailles begins to bombard Paris.
7 May	Free redemption of goods in pawn if the value less than 20 francs.
9 May	Fort d'Issy captured by Versailles troops. Delescluze made Delegate for War.
10 May	Versailles government signs peace treaty with Germany.
16 May	Vendôme Column demolished.
19 May	Church control over schools abolished.
21 May	Final full session of the Commune. Versailles troops enter Paris.
25 May	Depleted Commune meets for the last time. Delescluze dies on the barricades.
26 May	Commune executes hostages.
27 May	Mass executions of Communards begin at Père-Lachaise cemetery and continue for some days.
28 May	Last barricade captured. End of the Commune.
November	First death sentences at trials of Communards.
May **1872**	First deportation of Communard prisoners.
11 July **1880**	General Amnesty.

The Last Man on the Barricades

1

The man was alone on his side of the street barricade, shooting at the soldiers of the Versailles government. As he quickly loaded and reloaded his gun he was thinking about all that had happened and was happening in Paris. It was Sunday afternoon, 28 May 1871.

"Strange to be up here on this barricade. Alone too. Can't hear much shooting now. No you don't, soldier-boy. Scram with my bullet in your arm. Got to be careful. Not much ammunition left. Rest of Paris seems quiet – too quiet. Have those pigs from Versailles taken over then? Bang: another one for you, my French brother and enemy. Missed, but he's scuttled back like a squawking hen to his troop. Must reload. Never know when they are going to attack again.

"Quick, another couple of shots at their flag on that barricade down there. Just to keep them busy. Wonder what the time is? All the clocks here seem to have stopped. I'm hungry too. I've been on duty since dawn. Must be after midday. Got you, country boy; lie quiet, poor bastard.

"Where's everybody else? It's lonely standing here on these darned cobblestones. At least we know how to make barricades. I must hold on. Not be afraid. Maybe my comrades are regrouping – if we've anything left to fight with. Things look bad all round.

Communards fought street by
street to hold Paris

How long can we hold them back? They say over a hundred Communards were lined up against the cemetery wall this morning and shot down. No trial; nothing. Just shot. The bodies left barefoot; even in death somebody steals the rotten boots. Steady; aim carefully. Can't waste my few bullets. Good; that hit their flag again.

"Bloody shame. We started so full of hope last March. A world away now, but only two months really. Our own government, justice, sharing work and wages – that was our idea in the Commune. Now it's all smashed to pieces. Only a memory. Get back, soldier-boy; we Communards don't give up so easily after a week of fighting for our rights and our city. Got you in the leg, poor devil. You're one of us under the skin, only you don't know it. You've been lied to by the Versailles gang. It'll be back to the old ways, and no change for you or me. The bosses will come out on top again.

"Two shots left. Very quiet now. What's happening in the rest of Paris? Well, here goes. I'll send these with a '*Vive la Commune*'. That's stopped the bastards for the moment. Hell, I've nothing left to fight with. Must go now. Don't panic; mustn't run away. I'll leave as though strolling down the street so they think that there are still others on the barricade. There aren't, of course. Hope I don't get a goodbye bullet in the back. This is the end of the Commune for me."

And so he walked away. He was lucky: he was alive, unlike his other comrades. He was the last man on the last barricade. His name is unknown, but he held up

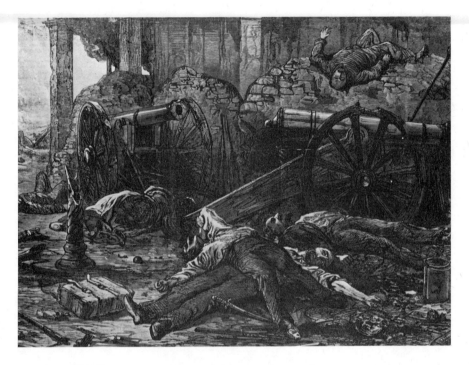

the Versailles troops in the rue Ramponneau for a quarter of an hour. If he had been caught, he would have been put on trial, or more probably shot against a wall. Instead he just melted away into the Paris streets; but his lone battle has gone down in history. In a way he speaks for all those other unknown Parisians who fought and died for their Commune in the early summer of 1871.

The Communards were pioneers opening up a new frontier. They wanted to make a better and more just society where everyone decided the laws and shared

The end of the Commune

the work and the wealth. A commune is an old form of city government in France, but this one was re-fashioned to fit human needs and socialist ideas. The Paris Commune grew out of a war and a siege, flowered briefly in hope, and died in a violent civil war seventy-two days after it began.

Paris at War

2

All the events in this story took place in Paris. The streets, parks and buildings of this compact and beautiful capital provided the stage for the drama of the Commune.

Great changes were made to the size and shape of the city under the Emperor Napoleon III (1852–1870), a nephew of the great Napoleon. He wanted to make Paris a modern and handsome capital for his Empire, so he put Baron Haussmann, a French architect, in charge of the planning and rebuilding. First the city boundaries were extended from 12 to 20 *arrondissements* (districts), and the Bois de Boulogne was turned from a forest into a landscaped public park. Then many of the old buildings and narrow medieval streets were torn down, and the famous network of sewers were built underground; these became, and remain, quite a tourist attraction. Above ground new and splendid buildings such as the Opera House, churches, the Halles Centrales, the Palais de Justice, railway stations, the bridges over the Seine, and great apartment blocks were built along broad modern streets (*boulevards*) radiating out from the Arc de Triomphe. It was said at the time that these wide streets would make it easier for the military to control crowds in riots. Altogether Haussmann demolished 24,404

overleaf: an aerial view of Paris

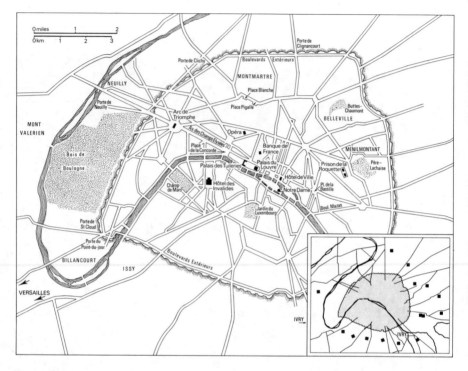

Paris 1871. Note the fortified wall and, inset, the ring of forts surrounding the city

houses and built 74,597 new ones. Gas lighting was one of the modern inventions introduced to make the city gay at night in this period of the can-can and the waltz.

But all this building and remodelling hit the working people of Paris. It meant that great numbers of them were dislodged from the centre of the city, where they had lived close to their work, because they could not afford the higher rents being charged for the new houses and flats. They had no choice but to move out to the fast-growing suburbs on the edge of Paris, such as Belleville and Ménilmontant. It was in neighbour-hoods like these as well as Montmartre and Montrouge that the workers were concentrated, and where the strongest support for the Commune would lie.

France had a population of around 37 million in 1870, with over a million and a half people living in Paris. Many of the workers came from the provinces to work in the capital in the new industries of engineering, chemicals, metallurgy and the railways. The others provided the traditional services as cobblers, tailors, printers, waiters, shopkeepers, building workers and domestic servants. At the same time, in this period of commercial and industrial expansion, the new middle classes grew in numbers and in power, and became the owners and controllers of banks and businesses. The French invented the name "bourgeoisie" for them.

But while the middle classes prospered, the working people were left behind. It is estimated that by 1870 rents had doubled, taking one-third of the average wage, while food cost 60 per cent of the weekly earnings, so there was not much left over to spend. This is

Railways were important in the expansion of Paris, creating new industries and jobs

one reason why pawnshops were so common, and why French working people began to eat horse meat because it was cheaper. So Paris was a city of showy contrasts: centre of fashion and slums, rich and poor, beggars and bankers, where one ball gown could cost twenty times the yearly wages of a working woman.

Paris is not only the centre of government and commerce. It has also been the centre for three revolutions – in 1789, 1830 and 1848 – when its citizens had actively helped to get rid of three kings. The first and most important of these, known as the French Revolution, had far-reaching effects throughout the world, and many

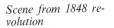
Scene from 1848 revolution

Emperor Louis-Napoleon and his family

of its ideals – "Liberty, Equality and Fraternity" – were to be revived again under the Paris Commune. The ordinary people of Paris did not like royal rulers in theory or in practice since they had done little to give citizens their liberties or to improve their working or living conditions. They hated the Emperor. On the one hand he allowed them the vote, but on the other he stifled the press, controlled the trades unions, and sent his police spies everywhere. There was, therefore, strong support for a republican government in which everyone could play a part.

By 1870 the Parisians were experiencing hardship

Defeated Louis-Napoleon is taken to meet Bismarck, the Prussian Prime Minister

Léon Gambetta proclaims the republic

once more. In that summer the Emperor had involved the French in an unnecessary war with Prussia. The Prussians invaded France, and soon proved themselves to be the superior force. The French army was under-manned, under-equipped and badly led. On Friday 2 September, after a decisive battle, the French troops surrendered at Sedan, a small town close to the Belgian frontier. The Emperor was taken prisoner, and abdicated. News of the defeat reached the Empress Eugénie on Saturday afternoon, and by Sunday morning the whole of Paris knew. People came out on to the streets wanting to know what was happening, and also wanting to make things happen. A large crowd gathered in front of the Hôtel de Ville (City Hall) where Parisians always go in times of crisis.

"Down with the Empire," roared the crowd.

Léon Gambetta, balancing on a window ledge, proclaimed the Republic amid cheers, and announced the setting up of a temporary government of National Defence. There was no time to have an election, and ministers of the ex-Imperial government did not want to hand over power to any revolutionaries. So it was quickly suggested to the crowd outside, that the National Assembly deputies for Paris should be the members of the new government. Enthusiastically the crowd shouted its agreement. Everyone had different ideas about the sort of republic they wanted, and in the excitement did not notice the lack of an agreed political programme. Likewise no-one paid much attention to what the rest of France was thinking or wanting. Only one thing was certain. The Parisians wanted to go on fighting. They were confident that the hated Prussian invader could be driven out of France if the government would put some good strong blood into the battle by calling up citizens to serve in the National Guard, the part-time civilian army.

Now the crowds surged towards the Tuileries. The imperial flag was still flying, and the Empress was still in residence. They pushed their way through the gardens, and into the palace itself. Joking, jostling, trampling and tearing, they flung down furniture, hangings and china, while outside people climbed ladders to remove all signs of the Empire from the walls of the building. The hated Empire was dead! Long live the Republic!

Hastily the Empress Eugénie slipped through a side door, and out into the street. Heavily veiled, she crossed Paris in an ordinary horse-drawn cab, and made her way to her American dentist. He smuggled

her out of the capital the next morning, and arranged her passage into exile in England.

The confidence and optimism of that September day was not enough. In the month that followed, the remaining French armies were defeated again and again. Gradually the Prussians moved closer to Paris and began to encircle the city.

Joyful crowds celebrate the collapse of the Empire

The Siege

3

There was a lot to be done in Paris before the Prussians cut the city off. For the time being everybody was too busy preparing for the expected attack to quarrel about politics. The 64 kilometres of fortified walls, 9 metres high, encircling Paris had to be strengthened. Outside these lay a chain of forts which needed to be repaired, and stocked with arms and soldiers. Parisians sometimes took a sightseeing ride on the train which ran round the inside walls carrying soldiers and supplies. They went to watch the work going on, and to see the training of the regular army and the citizen National Guard.

The National Guard had been set up in the great revolution of 1789. It consisted of volunteers who served under arms for short periods, usually for local defence purposes. Up to the 1870 war the Guardsmen had come mainly from the better-off classes. But now, due to anger at the Prussian occupation, the temporary government had been forced by public opinion to call up all able-bodied men to defend Paris. Being out of touch with popular opinion they were surprised at the large numbers of working people and small shopkeepers who had volunteered in order to have a crack at the enemy. The war had put a lot of people out of work, and the daily pay of a Guardsman – 1.50 francs

Morale was high as Parisians
prepared to defend their city

plus 75 centimes for his wife – was not only welcome, but vital to buy enough food for a family. Within a few weeks the National Guard had grown to 350,000 men, grouped in neighbourhood battalions. The National Guard was now larger than the regular army defending Paris. It was a mass army of semi-trained, armed citizens with an odd mixture of uniforms and out-of-date rifles, who did not trust the military authorities. Some of the battalions elected their own commanders, and loyalty to comrades and neighbourhood tended to come before obedience to headquarters.

Women too were attached to the National Guard as *cantinières*; they supplied food and drink to the soldiers on the battlefield as well as basic first aid. Normally four *cantinières* were allowed to each battalion, but in practice there were more, as many women went into battle with their men. They were very brave too, and many times picked up guns and went on fighting longer than the Guardsmen.

Of course the need for arms, ammunition and uniforms provided work for many of the unemployed, including women. Theatres were turned into hospitals, and extra factory space was found in house basements, as well as in the Louvre palace. By the end of the siege, the make-shift workshops had managed to produce 400 cannon all paid for by street collections.

Wine, wheat, root vegetables and animal feed as well as hay, coal and wood trundled into the city by train and cart. Cattle and sheep were herded into the public parks to provide fresh meat. One British observer described it: "As far as the eye can reach, over

Women enlisted as cantinières. An unflattering portrait by an artist of the time

Fresh poultry was on sale for those who could afford it

every open space, down the long, long avenue all the way to Longchamp itself, nothing but sheep, sheep, sheep!"

It was managed just in time. From 19 September, Paris was surrounded by the Prussians and the siege was under way. The Prussians thought it would be easy. They would simply wait and the Parisians would soon give in when their food and fuel ran out. The temporary government, without telling the public, wanted to agree peace terms as quickly as possible so that France could return to the business of making money and goods. But the Parisians were armed and eager to fight the enemy.

The city waited. The Prussians did not attack. Theatres, music halls and cafés were closed by ten o'clock every night as there was a curfew. The night life of the city, once so gay and alive, was now dark and dead. Paris began to feel cut off from the rest of France. What was going on? Was the country rearming against the invaders?

Identity card issued to Edwin Child, a young Englishman who wrote a diary of his experiences

Communications were cut: no post, no telegrams. Some news was received by carrier-pigeons bringing microfilm despatches from other parts of France. But this was not a reliable news service since only 59 pigeons out of the 392 sent off actually reached Paris. This was the first time that the camera had been used to photograph reports onto microfilm, which was then rolled up, and strapped to the pigeons' legs. At the receiving end the film was projected, and in the process enlarged, on to a wall by magic lantern.

To send messages out of the city, balloons were used which could fly people and despatches over the enemy lines. The Prussians were astonished, and only man-

Carrier-pigeons in the service of the Commune

PAR BALLON MONTÉ.

aged to shoot down 5 of the 65 manned balloons that left Paris during the four-and-a-half month siege. Gambetta, the Minister of the Interior, left in one of the first balloons in order to organize the armies in the south. The balloons were made of varnished cotton, filled with coal gas, and had a basket attached by ropes to the main balloon structure. The only trouble was that they were impossible to control. They went where the winds blew them – up and down, to Holland, Bavaria and once as far away as Norway.

For a time these activities cheered the besieged Parisians. Then at the end of October there was another French defeat at Metz. A month later, what was to have been a glorious attack on the Prussian lines by the National Guard ended in muddled retreat and defeat. It seemed that the Guards were no better trained than the regular army and that the government was not being serious about fighting the enemy.

A letter sent out of Paris by balloon post

30

By the beginning of December, in one of the coldest winters within living memory, food and fuel were running out. Everybody was waiting – waiting on guard duty on the city walls, waiting for the attack which never came, waiting in queues to buy food. There was no rationing, so the poor suffered greatly when the price of food rose, while the richer classes managed comfortably.

A sample of wages and food prices at the time shows these contrasts:

DAILY WAGES FOR MEN

Factory worker	3-6 francs
Transport worker	3-6 francs
Building worker	3-6 francs
General worker	2.50 francs
National Guard	1.50 francs
	(+ 75 centimes allowance for wife)

DAILY WAGES FOR WOMEN

Florist	2.25-3.50 francs
Washerwoman	2.25 francs
Milliner	1.50-2.25 francs
Dressmaker	1.00-2.25 francs
Domestic servants	These varied but were lower than wage of dressmaker

PRICES

Butter	20 francs a pound
Eggs	1 franc each
Rats	2-3 francs each
Dog	5-6 francs a pound
Elephant trunk	40 francs a pound

CARTE DE BOULANGERIE

Edwin Child's bread ration card

From 19 January ration cards were given out for the daily bread allowance: 300 grammes for adults, 150 grammes for children. The bread had straw and paper mixed in it.

People ate horse stew until they ran out of horses. It is estimated that 65,000 horses, 5,000 cats and 1,200 dogs were eaten during the siege. Rat hunts were a popular sport. The meat shortage got so bad that most of the animals at the zoo were killed off. One writer dined off camel, antelope, dog, donkey, mule and elephant of which, "I approve in the order written." But the poor could not afford such rare dishes.

One reporter saw a family of father, mother, and three children boiling a small lump of horsemeat, ten centimetres square, in a bucket to make a thin soup to last for three days. The day before, they had each had only one carrot to eat.

The cold was so piercing and the lack of fuel so great that people burnt furniture and the doors of empty houses, and cut down all the trees in the streets and parks. But green wood did not burn very well. Another way they kept warm was by wearing paper shirts.

The Prussians got tired of waiting around for Paris to give in, and began to bombard the city. The heavy shelling from the new Krupps siege guns went on night and day for three weeks. But the city did not give in. In fact people grew used to this new hazard. About a thousand buildings were damaged, but only 97 people were killed by direct hits.

Paris was beginning to look bleak under the winter skies, denuded of trees and horses, and with damaged buildings and dreary food queues. Young children were the first to die from hunger and cold. The novelist, Emile Zola wrote, "Paris without gas . . . shivering under an icy mantle, Paris whose black bread and horseflesh were doled out to her in infinitesimal quantities, continued hoping – despite everything." But hope did not prevent the deaths of 11,865 people in December and 19,233 in January 1871.

Queueing for food

The Parisians were getting angry with the temporary government. It seemed to be doing nothing about the siege. If there was an armed attack by the National Guard it was never properly planned or led. Many ordinary people, including the National Guard, started to discuss what ought to be done about the Prussian invaders, and what sort of reforms were wanted. Then they heard on 18 January that the German Empire had been proclaimed with the Prussian King as Emperor. The Parisians felt particularly insulted as the Germans had chosen to proclaim their new Empire at Versailles, a traditional symbol of French power and glory. Feelings ran high and there was talk of throwing out the government and setting up a Commune. Wall posters appeared publicly saying this. Twice some of the radical National Guard units had tried to take over the Hôtel de Ville, but had not succeeded.

Meanwhile the temporary government, while the public supported the war, was secretly negotiating an armistice with the Germans which was signed on 28 January. Paris felt betrayed, outraged. True, the siege was lifted after four-and-a-half months, and there was time to restock with food. But two bad things happened.

First, the government let the Germans celebrate their victory by coming into the city for two days at the beginning of March. All they could do was hang out black mourning drapes and shut the shops when the Germans came riding in. Then everybody came out to sweep and clean the streets so that all traces of the Prussian victory parade would be washed away.

German troops parade through Paris

Second, a new National Assembly was elected which was pro-royalist and unfriendly to Paris. It moved out of the city to Versailles because it thought the republican Parisians and the National Guard were too unruly and disrespectful, and that it was not safe in the capital. Adolphe Thiers was elected head of the government which was to draw up a peace treaty with the Germans. Worse blows followed. The Assembly voted to stop the pay of the National Guard, and ordered Parisians to repay their commercial debts and back rents. Owing to the war and the siege they had been allowed to hold these over because of hardship and unemployment. It was unfair. The Parisians felt they had suffered the worst of the war while the rest of France had got off lightly.

Takeover Day

4

Relations between the people of Paris and the new Thiers government were uneasy. Both sides were waiting to see what the other would do.

In the early hours of Saturday, 18 March, most people were still asleep. Up in the hilly village of Montmartre in the north of the city, government soldiers, under the command of General Lecomte, moved quietly to take over the cannon held by the National Guard. Thiers feared that the guns might be turned on his government forces down in Paris if the Guards rebelled. He did not trust them. By 4 a.m. the Guardsmen on duty, taken by surprise, had been overpowered and locked up in the cellars of a nearby restaurant. The guns had been captured and still the village slept on. But there was a hitch. The soldiers had forgotten to bring the horses needed to drag the guns, 250 of them, down the hill and across Paris. So the government soldiers, most of them young recruits, had to wait by the guns, stamping their feet for warmth, and hungry for their breakfast.

It so happened that Louise Michel, who was very active in socialist politics and known as "the red virgin", came to deliver a message to the National Guard in the district. She saw that one Guardsman had been wounded and thought that something was wrong.

Louise Michel

After giving him first aid, she ran into the streets to awaken the neighbourhood. Afterwards she wrote:

I went down, my rifle under my coat, crying "Treason".
A column was forming . . . Montmartre was waking.
The call to arms was sounding out. I was returning,
indeed, but with the others, to the attack on the heights
of Montmartre: we ran up at the double, knowing that
at the top there was an army in battle formation. We
expected to die for liberty. It was as if we were lifted
from the earth . . .

Awakened National Guards, half-dressed, ran out of the houses to join their local battalions. Women and children also came out into the streets to buy their bread and milk, and to get water from the village pumps. They joined the crowd gathering around the uneasy soldiers guarding the cannon. These were the cannon that had been paid for by the Parisians for use against the Germans.

The crowd appealed to the soldiers, calling them brothers, and saying, "You will not fire upon the people." The crush of the crowd became unbearable. The order was given to fire. The soldiers hesitated, and then most of them turned their rifles upside down with the butts in the air. They would no longer obey their officers and joined the crowd who embraced and cheered them. General Lecomte was then arrested by his own soldiers and marched off to a house in the rue des Rosiers. Later in the day he was joined by old General Clément Thomas, the unpopular ex-commander of the National Guard who was hated for his part in crushing the 1848 Revolution. The General had been recognized wandering around in civilian clothes.

At 10.30 a.m. three blank shots were fired from Montmartre to tell the rest of Paris that the guns were still theirs. Down below people were milling around in the streets asking one another what was going on. Some were busy tearing up the street cobblestones to build barricades to stop rush attacks by the regular soldiers. They were made from anything lying around: cobblestones, buses, carts, furniture, doors and so on.

The guns of Montmartre

The National Guard encouraged everyone to help build barricades

Soon all over the city the barricades appeared, and so did the crowds like sea waves mixing and moving between the red-trousered regular soldiers and the blue-uniformed National Guard. It was confusing. Nobody seemed to be in charge or to know what was happening. The National Guard marched around and took some prisoners. The regular soldiers would face them at one moment and then disappear. Later it was learned that they were retreating to their barracks.

In the Place Pigalle a large crowd from the poorest districts was pushing and chivvying the soldiers. There was some scuffling and then shooting. An army captain on a white horse tried to ride into the crowd, but he and his horse were shot down. Half an hour later only the bones of the horse remained. Local women had stripped off the still warm flesh to provide meat for their families. This was a skill they had learned during the recent siege.

On the Bastille Column – sited where the first revolution had started in 1789 – a red flag was flying in place of the national tricolour.

By midday the traffic had just about stopped and many shops were closing. People went off to eat. In the lull photographers became busy taking posed pictures of proud Guardsmen at the barricades. They were using big box-shutter cameras which were heavy to handle. It was a slow business as you had to remain still for a long time until the camera clicked the picture.

That afternoon the streets were crowded again. Everybody was curious and uncertain. But there was a feeling of change in the air. Sometimes you heard shouts of *"Vive la République"* and *"Vive la Commune"*. At one moment in the Place Bastille there was a roll of drums, the National Guard presented arms and the crowd parted respectfully as a funeral procession moved past. Behind the coffin, hatless and in a black cloak, walked the famous old radical poet, Victor Hugo. He was on his way to Père-Lachaise cemetery to bury his son, who had died a few days earlier. It was a moving sight: the makers of a new revolution saluted the poet who had fought for the republic in the previous revolutions.

Meanwhile up in Montmartre the crowds were becoming more excited and angry, demanding the execu-

A reconstructed photograph of the execution of the generals

tion of the two prisoner generals. National Guard officers tried to protect them as prisoners of war, and planned to smuggle them to safety when darkness fell. However the crowd became uncontrollable, and stormed the small house in the rue des Rosiers where the generals were held as prisoners of war. They rushed the generals into the garden and shot them without ceremony. Clément Thomas had 70 bullets in his body. This was the first brutality in what was to become a civil war of great cruelty.

Down in the city, Thiers realized that he had lost control of the situation. He had no more than 6,000 loyal National Guards to maintain order. So when a number of radical National Guards came to the Hôtel de Ville that afternoon, Thiers ordered the government to withdraw to Versailles. In haste and confusion government members escaped down back stairs, through underground passages, and even out of windows. They dashed away in carriages to the safety of Versailles. Nobody stopped them. Indeed few realized they had gone.

Not until late in the evening did a former army officer, later known as "Burner" Brunel, enter the Hôtel de Ville. He found it empty. People knew Paris was theirs when the special gas flares lit up the front of the Hôtel de Ville, and they saw a red flag flying from its belfry. What a day! No-one had any idea when it started that the National Guard and the citizens would have taken Paris by the time it ended.

Adolphe Thiers

The Commune

5

Suddenly, joyfully, Paris felt free. It was not mob control but practical co-operation between the National
Guard and the ordinary citizens. City life was nearly
normal except that it was now much more exciting.
Shops and cafés were open, newspapers appeared –
even those of the opposition – and the streets were
swept. There was less crime, and no looting; the
National Guard were again paid regularly out of public funds, and relief (food and money) for the poor
continued to be given out at the local town halls. However many of the better-off residents fled in panic to
Versailles or the countryside, "not liking the control
of workmen" as de Goncourt wrote in his Journal.
During this period an estimated 80,000 to 100,000
people left Paris. Those who remained had nowhere
else to go and were tied to their work in the city. But
now, after work, they would join the crowds in the
streets to watch all that was going on, and to discuss
the news and future changes they were going to make.
At times of political change – revolutionary change
like this one – people always come out of their private
shells into the public life of the community. They again
greeted one another with the title of "citizen", as they
had done during other revolutions; gone were the
forms of address denoting rank and class.

Twenty-three kilometres away at Versailles, the Thiers government waited and watched, expecting the breakdown of law and order. It was fed by reports from secret agents who slipped in and out of Paris since there were no security checks. Others also went to and fro to try and make the peace between Paris and Versailles, but without success. No agreement was

The guns of Fort Valérien trained on Paris

reached between the French at Versailles and the French in Paris. And all the time the German army remained, partly surrounding Paris, watching events.

The elections for the Commune were held on 26 March. Versailles said they were illegal and asked people not to vote. Everybody in Paris took part in the elections, though only men had the vote. The Central Committee of the National Guard gave some practical advice to the voters on wall posters:

Citizens,
Remember that the men who still serve you best are those whom you will choose from among your own ranks, who lead the same lives as yourselves and suffer the same hardships . . .
Beware of the ambitious and the newly rich . . .
Beware, too, of wind-bags who prefer words to deeds . . . And avoid those whom fortune has favoured excessively. The wealthy are rarely disposed to considering the working classes as their brothers . . .

Two days later in a simple ceremony in front of the Hôtel de Ville the Commune was proclaimed. The newly elected members, following the 1789 tradition, wore red sashes as the symbol of the people's government and with the red flag waving over their heads, took the salute at a march past of the National Guard to the sound of drums and bands, gun salvoes and the cheers of the great crowds. They shouted *"Vive la Commune"* because for the first time the government *was* the people. The members were their neighbours and friends with whom problems and ideas could be discussed freely.

Jules Vallès, a member of the Commune, wrote in his newspaper *Le Cri du Peuple*, on 30 March:

Today is the festive wedding day of the Idea and the Revolution. Soldier-citizens, the Commune we have acclaimed and married today must tomorrow bear fruit; we must take our place once more, still proud and now free, in the workshop and at the counter. After the poetry of triumph, the prose of work.

One of the unique things about the Commune was that nearly a third of the 90 members were working class. It was the first time that workers had been elected freely to make the policies instead of having to endure them. After all, at that period in the nineteenth century, nobody with power or wealth in Europe or America thought workers had a right to share in a country's government. They were there to do the work for as low a wage as possible – one which would just keep them from starving – so that the profits could be as high as possible.

The other difference was that there were no organized political parties as there are today. They were all socialists at heart, although some were less revolutionary than others. They were agreed that government should be by and for the people; that property and profits should be shared; and that there should be social justice for all. Of course they talked and argued a lot about the different kinds of socialism and how it should be applied. Some of these loose groupings were called the Jacobins, Blanquists and Communists. But they were all Communards and only a small group were Communists.

The work of the Commune itself was done by committees who elected Delegates as leaders or ministers of government departments.

The Communards rejoiced when they heard that other cities in France had also set up Communes: Lyons, Marseilles, Toulouse, Narbonne, St. Etienne, Le Creusot, and Limoges. They hoped that France could be governed in the future by independent city communes elected by local citizens, all linked together in a national federation of the United Communes of France. But this did not happen. All these other communes were quickly crushed by the Versailles government.

Indeed it was hard for the Paris Commune's news and views to get through to the rest of the country. Thiers put a news barrier round Paris and only let other Frenchmen read or hear his version of events. Today this would be called propaganda. So most of France was led to believe that the Communards were bloodthirsty red rebels out to crush civil liberties and all private property.

The Commune's most pressing problem was survival, and this meant military survival first. But the trouble with the Communards was that they were so busy planning social reforms that they never got to grips with the Versailles government. They should have marched there in the first few weeks and forced Thiers to make an agreement. And if they had thought of taking control of the Bank of France in Paris which held the country's gold reserves, that might have given them a bargaining counter with which to persuade

The National Guard leave Paris for Versailles

Versailles to allow them to have their own form of self-government. The Commune had the arms and the men. Thiers did not at first. In fact he had to play for time and get the Germans to allow him to recruit and train a new French army. Once Paris was retaken he told them, then France would get on with the peace treaty. He had no doubts. It was civil war.

As it turned out the Commune was not really prepared for civil war and military planning, so it did not train the National Guard nor prepare the defences of

Paris very efficiently. The three Commanders-in-Chief, Lullier, Cluseret and Rossel who were professional soldiers, lasted about seven weeks altogether in command. They were frustrated by the lack of a clear military policy and the democratic dilly-dallying. In addition, they were too impatient with the civilian spirit of the time, and not all that experienced as military leaders.

The Commune was so democratic that it was often difficult to be effective. Every member always had a chance to state his views. The National Guard also discussed policies and military orders before carrying them out. This was admirable but not always practical. It is not practical when you have an enemy – the Versailles government – preparing to attack as soon as they are strong enough.

The one big attack against the Versailles forces on 3–4 April, which the Commune confidently expected to win, ended in muddle and retreat. Three National Guard columns started out so jauntily and confidently with all Paris cheering them on. But there turned out to be no plan of action and no communication between the columns. They were outflanked by the Versailles armies, and in spite of brave fighting, had to surrender or retreat into Paris. It made Parisians weep to see them straggling back in small groups, tired, wounded and dirty; all the glory knocked out of them.

But worse news was to follow. Versailles lost 25 killed and 125 wounded, while the Commune had an enormous number killed and 1,200 prisoners taken. These prisoners were spat upon, cursed and beaten by

Women beg for news of prisoners held in Versailles

the so-called "respectable" citizens of Versailles. This was the first time that the Communards realized how much they were hated by the bourgeoisie. Many Communards were taken prisoner and shot without mercy on the battlefield. One of the Commune's military heroes, Flourens, had his head smashed in by a policeman's sabre while resting at an inn. His body was sent in a dung cart to Versailles to be identified. And the Communard general, Duval, was just shot on the spot where he surrendered. The official Versailles report said, "another of their generals, Duval, was killed by our men at the moment of assault."

One month later relations between the last Commander-in-Chief, Rossel, the best of the soldiers left, and the National Guard were bad. On 7 May Rossel ordered an attack to relieve Fort d'Issy. Only 7,000 Guards out of the promised 12,000 turned up to fight. The next day he resigned in disgust. The old revolutionary leader, Delescluze, became the new Delegate for War. But despite the fact that he had fought in the 1848 revolution he was not a trained military man; the National Guards were now under civilian leadership.

Charles Delescluze

A selection of Commune newspapers

Citizens Committed

6

The people of Paris made the Commune. The Commune gave a lot of ordinary citizens the confidence to do things together that they would never have dared to do before – or have been allowed to do. Other countries with less democratic governments found the Commune alarming and, not surprisingly, the Communards got a very bad press outside. For example the London *Times* reported on 7 April 1871, "The men of the Commune do not intend to be disappointed. They have promised themselves to annihilate Paris, its fortunes, its commerce, its population – and they keep their word. Never was the work of destruction carried on with a more wicked and brutal perseverance." Communards were branded as "the mob, red insurgents, bandits, anarchists, convicts, scum, moral gangrene, socialists". Socialist was a dirty word then.

As usually happens in times of political change, a lot of new newspapers were rushed into print. But not everyone knew how to read them. The most direct way of taking part in Commune affairs was by joining one of the many political clubs. These were a tradition of revolutionary Paris, and had been revived during the siege. Their activities were often held in churches as these were the largest and most convenient local meeting places. People would hurry there after work to discuss the issues of the day. As the Communal Club of 111 Arrondissement pointed out:

> Follow our example; open Communal clubs in all the churches. The priests can conduct services in the daytime and you can provide the people with political education in the evenings.

Here is another wall poster, signed by a Jules Morelly:

> Citizens ... It is only at public meetings that we are able to enlighten ourselves regarding the stormy times through which we are passing. We thus request your presence and participation, in order that each citizen know fully what is occurring, how it is occurring and how it ought to occur ...

Communards used churches for meetings

All sorts of subjects were discussed in the clubs –
the position of the wealthy, the priests, prostitution,
the equality of women, the abolition of marriage, how
to win the civil war and what social reforms were
needed. People argued and shouted a lot at each other,
and sometimes the ideas put forward were crazy, but
most of the time the discussions were serious and
practical. Women were particularly active in the clubs.
They really enjoyed the freedom, and, for the first
time, were not afraid to speak in public. Listen to this
unknown woman speaker at a club meeting in the
Trinity church:

> . . . Yes, you women are oppressed. But have just a little
> more patience, for the day that will bring justice and
> satisfaction for our demands is rapidly approaching.
> Tomorrow you will belong to yourselves and not to
> exploiters. The factories in which you are crowded
> together will belong to you; the tools placed in your
> hands will belong to you; the profit that results from
> your labour, your care, and the loss of your health, will
> be shared among you . . .

Citizeness Valentin, speaking in the Club of the Pro-
letarians, proposed that women should, "Guard the
gates of Paris while the men go to battle."

There was not much time for private life. On top of
people's daily work there were meetings to attend,
ideas to put to Commune members, and the trades
unions to be got going again or new ones formed. By
the middle of May there were about 90 trades unions,
including women's ones, active in Paris.

One of the new ideas to change the system of work

was the concept of workers' co-operatives. These would give people more control over their working lives. Everyone who worked in a factory or machine shop would be in charge of running the business, making the goods and sharing out the profits once the expenses had been paid. This was felt to be a good way of getting rid of bosses, low wages and unfair differences between people. The problem was that ordinary workers had no money to invest in these co-operatives. But the Commune helped financially and soon there were 43 such co-operatives working in the city. This was quite an achievement for such a radical and new way of running industry.

The factory co-operative at the Louvre arms workshop functioned in the following way. The manager, shop foreman and chargehand were elected by all the workers. They had a Council meeting every day after the shift ended at 5.30 p.m. to discuss the day's work, and any reports and suggestions from within the factory. Each work-bench elected a delegate to the Council, and a new election was held every fortnight, so there was always a change round of delegates. Members of the Council could look at the account books at any time and information was not kept secret. Furthermore nobody could be dismissed unless the Council agreed. The working day was ten hours, from 7 a.m. to 6 p.m. with a lunch break from 11 a.m. to noon and the workers agreed that the wages should be as follows: Manager – 250 francs a month; Shop Foreman – 210 francs a month; Chargehand – 7 francs daily; Worker – 5–6 francs daily.

The Commune also agreed that workers' co-operatives could take over workshops and factories abandoned by their owners who had fled from Paris. The owners were to be paid compensation for them; it was not to be state control but workers' control. But this idea never got beyond the paper planning stage as there was no time to put it into practice before the Commune was defeated.

The bakers, whose work was hard, asked that night work be abolished, and the Commune agreed. This was good for the bakers, but not always convenient for the rest of the population who missed the freshly-baked bread in the mornings. Working people were also consulted about other laws to improve working

Street poster to announce enforcement of ban on night work for bakers

Costumes worn by women active in the defence of the Commune

and living conditions, which gave them the confidence to insist that the rights of labour were equal to those of private property.

One of the noticeable developments was the way in which women threw themselves into working for the Commune. They smelled liberation in the air. They felt the Commune would free them as well as their menfolk. In the nineteenth century women were expected only to work at home looking after the family, or, if they had to earn a living, to work quietly and obediently in low-paid jobs. Even some socialists thought that it was a woman's duty to be subservient to men. Women had few legal rights and no vote.

During the Commune women were active everywhere: in the political clubs, fighting alongside the National Guard, in their own trades unions and workers' co-operatives. In many battles the *cantinières* stayed behind to rescue the wounded, or to pick up a gun and blast away at the enemy. There was a women's battalion of the National Guard which put up a brave defence of the barricades in the last week of the Commune. Women fought like tigers released from a cage. They had so much to lose if the Commune went down.

Women worked with men on public committees, which they had not done before. At times they were also more far-sighted than the men. One of their strongest organizations, the Association of Women for the Defence of Paris and Aid to the Wounded, proposed, "variety of work in each trade; a reduction in working hours; an end to all competition between male and female workers – their interests are identical; equal

Some of the women active in the Commune

pay for equal hours of work . . ." They could see the dangers of rivalry between men and women to the Commune; it could divide them when the Communards needed to be united to make a better world.

In other ways women were full of energy and ideas. One group, seeing that girls were not given training for skilled work, proposed to set up an industrial training school for them. This was daring as there were not many training schools for boys at this time. Another group of women, determined that children should not suffer because their mothers had to work, produced a practical plan for day nurseries. These nurseries were to be near the large factories in light and airy houses, with child-size furniture, and plenty of toys and books to encourage them to play and use their imaginations. At the time this was quite a new and revolutionary approach to the problem of working mothers with children.

Inspired by the possibilities opened up by the Commune ordinary people in streets and neighbourhoods became involved in working for the community. People felt they were not wasted.

The Commune at Work

7

Because it was in close contact with ordinary people, the Commune really was a new kind of government. It wanted to make a new society which was not based on who were the bosses or who had the most money or who inherited the most property. As Jules Vallés, the Commune leader said: "The important thing is to explain what we would like, since we cannot do what we want."

Sometimes the Commune was in a muddle as to whether it was the government of France or only the government of Paris. It would pass a law but lack the power to enforce it anywhere other than in Paris. For example, they wanted to try and get rid of Church control of education, and the use of religion to stop people from improving their lives, and so they passed a law making the Catholic Church no longer part of the state. This meant that schools were no longer obliged to teach religious knowledge, and the influence of the Church on people's lives generally was weakened. The Church believed in making people ready for the next life, whereas the Commune believed in improving conditions in the life of the moment. They said: "What is the good of a better life after death? We want it now."

The Commune did not have long to carry out its

"Paris was never so quiet"! The
Commune viewed from Versailles

policies – only 72 days. And it was learning as it went along. Usually people did not bother much with governments. But this one was theirs so they were interested in everything it did.

Parisians were pleased, for instance, that the Commune decided to allow a three year period to pay the rents and bills which were owing because of the war, the siege and unemployment at the time. This helped the working people and the small shopkeepers. The National Assembly at Versailles had tried to make them pay up in early March when many had no wages and the National Guard had had their daily pay abolished. The Versailles rulers did not seem to understand how the ordinary people of Paris had suffered in the fight against the Germans.

Another change was that everybody who worked in the public services – in politics, the law courts or the civil service – had to be elected by popular vote to these jobs. In other words the electors were their masters and chose whether to elect or re-elect them. The Commune also set the top salary for all members of the government and the civil service at 6,000 francs a year, about double the pay of a skilled worker. This was a very radical decision at that time when the classes were separated economically and socially far more rigidly than today. It began the process of levelling out incomes.

One feature of poverty and low wages is the pawnshop. Many Parisians, who were out of work due to the war and the siege, had been forced to pawn their tools or household goods. They had no money to get them out of pawn again. Early in May the Commune allowed the free withdrawal of such goods worth up to twenty francs in value. It covered bedding, tools and books – there was some argument as to whether books could be claimed as tools – clothing, furniture, and linen. The pawnshop owners were to be paid out of public funds.

On 10 April the Commune formally adopted the widows and children of all National Guardsmen killed in battle. They would be given a state pension, whether they had been legally married to the Guardsmen or not. A lot of the Parisian working-class were not officially married according to the law or the Church, but couples had lived together faithfully. The Church and Versailles thought this reform was immoral and an attack upon the family.

One very important issue when building a new and just society is education. Eugène Vaillant, the Delegate for Education, wanted, "A reform of the educational system that will afford every individual the foundations for social equality." The long term aim was free and compulsory education for every boy and girl, with schools teaching science and practical subjects instead of the church catechism. There was not much money for an immediate change. Meetings were held with teachers and parents to discuss the reforms needed in the primary schools – a new approach in itself – and then a Commission was set up to put them into practice. The Commune did not know how little time they had left for such a major reform. It did however manage to re-open many schools to take in the

RÉPUBLIQUE FRANÇAISE

N° 59.

LIBERTÉ — ÉGALITÉ — FRATERNITÉ

N°

COMMUNE DE PARIS

LA COMMUNE DE PARIS,

Considérant que le premier des principes de la République française est la liberté

Considérant que la liberté de conscience est la première des libertés;

Considérant que le budget des cultes est contraire au principe, puisqu'il impose les citoyens contre leur propre foi;

Considérant, en fait, que le clergé a été le complice des crimes de la monarch contre la liberté,

DÉCRÈTE :

ART. 1er. L'Eglise est séparée de l'État.

ART. 2. Le budget des cultes est supprimé.

ART. 3. Les biens dits de mainmorte, appartenant au congrégations religieuses, meubles et immeubles, son déclarés propriétés nationales.

ART. 4. Une enquête sera faite immédiatement sur ce biens, pour en constater la nature et les mettre à la dis position de la Nation.

LA COMMUNE DE PARIS

Paris, le 3 avril 1871.

IMPRIMERIE NATIONALE. — Avril 1871.

L'ignorance c'est l'esclavage — L'instruction c'est la liberté

thousands of children running around the streets because of the upsets of the siege. But there was a shortage of teachers when the priests were expelled.

In May the first technical school was opened. Some communal libraries, too, were established, and reading rooms in the hospitals. Free clothing, food and school materials were provided for poor children.

The Commune's work also reached out to the arts. Two days before the Versailles troops entered Paris, they were debating whether there should be state censorship of the theatres. One of the members said, "One is perfectly entitled to keep an eye on the way people use their minds, but to instruct them how to use them is a form of tyranny which is not only intolerable but fatal to the development of thought." Like so many other things, the Commune never had time to settle this important difference of principle: whether state censorship is necessary to build a new socialist society, or whether freedom in the arts is a vital defence against dictatorship in any society. Instead they compromised. The theatres could run themselves as co-operatives, and the police would not be used as censors unless the plays were considered immoral or dangerous.

Poster announcing Commune's position with respect to the Church

69

Festivals and Funerals

8

The Commune was not only work and reform. It was also gay and festive. People were living in a springtide of hope when everything seemed possible. The famous painter, Courbet, who was an elected member of the Commune, wrote to his parents, "I'm enchanted. Paris is a veritable paradise; no police, no outrages, no quarrels, no exactions of any kind. Paris is moving under its own steam as smoothly as you could wish. We must try and always be like this. . . ."

The streets hummed with life. People everywhere were talking, joking, reading the news, drinking, watching the life around them, and in friendly contact with each other. Shops, brothels and cafés did plenty of business as most people had jobs now, and there were no food shortages. In the evenings there were the queues for the theatres and music halls. People hurried off to attend their club meetings, which had become part of the new awareness. National Guardsmen marched by to the sound of military bands as did groups of workers with banners and flags. There were many public ceremonies to watch, though sadly these were all too often the funerals of Communards killed in the continuing civil war. War and pleasure spiced the air with excitement.

One poet wrote of this time:

Cantinière distributing refreshments

71

Would you believe it? Paris is fighting and singing! . . . No better reply could be made to our stubborn enemies' ceaseless cannonade than the refrain that a thousand voices intone every night in the twenty music halls of Paris,

> *The peoples of the world*
> *are brothers to us.*
> *Our enemies are the*
> *Versaillais*

In the background all the time was the continuous bombardment of the city by the heavy guns of Versailles. But even this soon became just part of normal daily life. It did not take long before the street sellers were out selling the shrapnel pieces as souvenirs. And still the German armies remained, half surrounding the city, watching. Parisians had almost forgotten that they were there. The fight was with Versailles now. Some parts of Paris, like Neuilly and Passy, were in ruins. Many street fronts gaped open with cannon shot. In the area around the Champ de Mars, where a powder magazine had been blown up by a gun shell, many houses looked like black skeletons.

Of course not everyone was in sympathy with the Communard way of life. Edmond de Goncourt wrote in his Journal on 28 April, "Weary of the spectacle of the street, of dirty, drunken National Guards, of toughs in full flower, I take refuge in the Zoo. . . ." And on 19 May, just before the fall of the Commune, he describes the scene from his point of view, in black despair, "all the people you meet in the street talk to themselves aloud like crazy people – people from whose mouths come words like *desolation, misfortune, death, ruin* – all the syllables of despair." This was the attitude common among the better-off middle classes who were discomfited by the Commune, and fearful for their property. For them law and order had broken down, and life was no longer predictable.

Expecting to be attacked by the Versailles armies, people became used to the barricades straddling the streets. The Committee of Public Safety, in its last proclamation on 24 May when the Versaillais were fighting their way through Paris, urged, "Let Paris bristle with barricades, and behind these improvised ramparts let our war cry ring out against the enemy . . . for thanks to its barricades Paris is impregnable." This was a bit romantic; however bravely the barricades were defended they could only hold up the advance of soldiers, not defeat them.

Rossel, the former Communard military leader, described the barricade fighter with admiration:

> Because he wants to be able to retreat easily the soldier of the barricades will not wear a uniform when he intends to engage in serious fighting. It may seem paradoxical, but the uniform does in fact lessen the street fighter's courage; men in overalls have far more energy, initiative and military skill than National Guardsmen, and especially officers of the National Guard.

The walls of the city were splashed with a variety of coloured posters. The Commune used these as a quick way of spreading news, views and new decrees. Somebody estimated that 395 official statements were posted up on the walls during the months of the Commune.

overleaf: building up the barricades

Overturned vehicles, cobblestones and rubble were used to reinforce barricades

Then there were also the separate posters and notices of the clubs, trades unions and local groups. A poster might ask citizens to build barricades in a couple of districts and offer them four francs a day as pay. Sometimes there was the odd Versailles poster calling on the citizens to give up and surrender. This latter kind would get a curse or a rude joke.

Flags and banners were seen everywhere in the processions of National Guardsmen, workers, clubs and other local groups. The colour red for revolution blazed out. Red flags flew on public buildings, appeared in processions and on the barricades, and were draped over the coffins of dead Communards. Women wore red shawls, often pistols were stuck into the belts. The red wine flowed too. Even the National Guard trained with crates of wine nearby. Disapprovingly de Goncourt noted, "all you see are National Guards rolling barrels to their posts, and the troops as they go out to seek glory are always accompanied by carts sagging under the weight of casks." The wine was cheap and a comfort, but not good for discipline.

Black was the other dominant colour, always reminding the Parisians of those being killed in the civil war. There were funerals every day. The Commune made great efforts to give all Guardsmen killed in battle a ceremonial burial: black-plumed horses, flags on the coffins and military guards of honour.

Popular concerts were held in the former royal palace of the Tuileries which was now open to the public. Soldiers, citizens and the wounded came to enjoy themselves and forget about the bombardment. An ex-army officer, Louis Barron, describes one of these Sunday concerts where the popular singer, La Bordas, "magnificent in her flowing robes draped with a scarlet sash", sang the hit song *La Canaille* (The Scum). And the audience joined in the chorus:

> *They're the scum!*
> *Well, I'm one of them.*

There were also other special events, symbolic of Communard ideals and feelings. One writer has called them "the language of acts". The burning of a new model of the guillotine in front of the statue of the famous writer Voltaire was one of these special occa-

Gustave Courbet, the painter, was held responsible for the destruction of the Vendôme Column. The faked photograph (bottom right) shows him apparently shaking hands with the demolition team

sions. It was meant to show popular disapproval of the death penalty and the use of the guillotine for execution by the Versailles government.

The most famous event was the pulling down of the Vendôme Column, originally built by Napoleon to commemorate his victories. For the Commune, as for all republicans and socialists, the column was, as the decree of 12 April said, "a monument of barbarism, a symbol of brute force and false glory, an affirmation of militarism . . ." The destruction of the column on 16 May became a public festival. Crowds turned out to watch the event set for 2 p.m. They waited cheerfully but at the first attempt at 3.30 p.m. only the capstan broke, not the column. There were cries of "treachery". The crowds went on waiting, listening to the bands. After rush repairs and two hours later, the cables attached to the column were tightened. There was a "huge zig-zag through the air . . . a cloud of smoke" and the column lay split into pieces on the ground. The Communards had shown their break with past imperial glories. Later that day the Place Vendôme was renamed the Place Internationale.

The Versailles leaders were shocked at this example of unpatriotic behaviour, this denial of French military virtues. Later, when they came back to power they tried to make Courbet, the painter, pay to replace the column. The cost was approaching 550,000 francs. Courbet, who had not taken part in the decision to pull the column down, and who had no money, was forced to flee to Switzerland to avoid paying.

The Week of Blood

9

The civil war between Frenchmen and Frenchmen was bitter and cruel. This is always the worst kind of war. You have only to remember the civil war in England in the seventeenth century, or the one in America in the nineteenth, to understand. When both sides are fighting for ideas that they believe in they show little mercy to one another.

The Thiers government feared that Paris's demand for self-government would lead to the break-up of the French state, particularly if the idea of independent Communes spread to other towns. They were also afraid of the socialist reforms of the Commune. These would destroy their comfortable bourgeois business society, based on private property and backed by the Church. In addition the members of the National Assembly came from the Catholic conservative countryside and provinces. They were deeply suspicious of the republicans, "the new barbarians" from the capital, and thought they were godless socialists who would destroy law and order. They called for public prayers to show the world that "France recognizes at last the only hand which can heal and save it." The attitude of the army officers towards the Commune is shown in the statement to the press made by General de Gallifet, "It is war without truce or pity that I de-

The Archbishop of Paris

clare on these assassins." So Versailles would not grant Paris any form of self-government. Neither would Thiers agree to exchange one of the socialist leaders, Blanqui, whom he held prisoner, for the Archbishop of Paris, whom the Communards were holding as a hostage.

The Versaillais had the support of the Germans for this policy. The German leaders saw the Commune as a threat to all established governments. They were afraid that the social ideas of a working class in charge might spread throughout Europe. Therefore they allowed Thiers to raise a new French army, and to move it through their lines in order to attack Paris.

The Commune was having a meeting on the Sunday evening of 21 May when they were interrupted by the shocking news that the Versailles troops had entered Paris by the Saint-Cloud Gate.This was around 7 p.m. An hour later the final Commune session ended. They left no committees behind to direct the defence of the city. Only Delescluze, the civilian Delegate for War, remained at the Hôtel de Ville.

The only advice given to the citizens of Paris was the traditional one of fighting behind the barricades. Delescluze sent out this appeal:

> Enough of militarism, no more staff officers with gold-embroidered uniforms! Make way for the people, the bare-armed fighters! The hour of revolutionary war has struck. The people know nothing of elaborate manoeuvres, but when they have a rifle in their hands and cobblestones under their feet, they have no fear of the strategists of the monarchist school.

Entry at St-Cloud

This turned out to mean that there was to be no centrally organized defence, and that officers' orders were no longer obeyed. It was every neighbourhood, every street, every man and woman for themselves.

The surprisingly easy entry of the Versailles forces into Paris was due to chance. A civil engineer taking his Sunday afternoon walk noticed that the Saint-Cloud Gate was undefended. He waved a cloth to attract the attention of the nearby Versailles soldiers, who were not expecting to attack the city for another two days. A message was sent to Thiers who arrived in time to see his freshly-trained troops quietly enter an unresisting city. Once within the walls the Versailles

forces split into two columns. The strategy was the pincer one of two arms squeezing in towards the centre of Paris. By 1 a.m. the next morning the Trocadéro had been captured and became the army headquarters. They had advanced much faster than planned, and had to stop to let their supplies catch up with them.

The Versaillais moved forward into the city very cautiously as they did not know how strong the resistance would be. On the Commune side all seemed to be confusion at the command level. Orders and counter-orders flowed from the Hôtel de Ville, the Committee of Public Safety and the National Guard Central Committee. Delescluze, already worn out with consumption but still the optimistic revolutionary of 1848, sat in his office signing orders which were never delivered and never obeyed since no-one had authority now. Appeals were made to the Versailles soldiers to lay down their arms and join their fellow workers, without success. Passers-by in the streets were pressed into helping to build hasty barricades.

In the middle were the turncoats who were getting tricolour armlets and flags ready to replace the red ones when the Versaillais reached their district. Some frightened people tried to escape through the German lines. But the German army, by agreement with Thiers, closed this escape route.

It was a desperate situation, but one where Parisians fought well on their own territory. Eye witnesses reported many acts of bravery by unknown men and women.

In the newspaper kiosk at Montparnasse station a

Bitter fighting on the barricades

Communard worker held out alone after his comrades had retreated, firing at the enemy until his ammunition ran out.

An American watched:

> a young and apparently goodlooking woman spring upon the barricade, a red flag in her hand, and wave it defiantly at the troops. She was instantly shot dead.

De Goncourt described a scene in which a lieutenant of the National Guard, with bullets flying around him, tried to carry away a dead comrade. He was shot in the thigh which "made them turn together in a hideous pirouette, the dead man and the living man, and fall on top of each other. I doubt that many people have been privileged to witness so heroic and simple a disdain for death."

The 120-strong women's battalion defended the barricade in the Place Blanche until they were forced to retreat to the Place Pigalle. Here they fought until they were surrounded. Their commander, who was a bricklayer, was shot on the spot by a Versailles officer who sneered, "Oh, so bricklayers are to be the commanders now." The remainder of the women who got away retreated to the Boulevard Magenta, where not one of them survived the fighting.

The fighting was vicious. The French fought more fiercely against each other than they had done against the German invaders nine months before. On the whole the Communards did not shoot prisoners in cold blood. Only 183 Versaillais were reported as missing in the period of the Commune. And of the 300

hostages held in Paris, only 63 were shot in cold blood in the last week of the Commune when people got desperate and did not obey the law. The execution of the Archbishop of Paris, who was being held hostage, and the random shooting of some innocent Dominican monks in the street shocked the world and did much to damage the name of the Commune.

Although Thiers had said there would be no retaliation except according to the law, prisoners from the barricades were rarely left alive. They were lined up against a wall or railing and shot. General de Gallifet lined up prisoners in the Bois de Boulogne and picked out those who had watches, grey hair or faces he did not like. These were executed on the spot. When the Versaillais finally captured Montmartre they picked at random 42 men, 3 women and 4 children, took them

Another photographic reconstruction: the shooting of the Dominican monks

The Versailles army round up suspects

to the rue des Rosiers where the two generals had been executed, and shot them.

One American observer saw the bodies of six children lying in the Avenue d'Autin, "the eldest apparently not over fourteen, shot to death . . ." Even the conservative London *Times*, of 29 May, and no friend of the Commune, protested about "the inhuman laws of revenge under which the Versailles troops have been shooting, bayonetting, ripping up prisoners, women and children during the last six days . . . So far as we can recollect there has been nothing like it in history." Twenty thousand Parisians were killed in that one week.

The desire for revenge even infected those respectable Parisians who were relieved at the arrival of the Versailles army. Well-dressed women poked at the bodies of dead Communards, tipped the caps off their faces, spat on and insulted them. Often the dead had the clothes and boots ripped off them.

The intensity of the street fighting was heightened by great fires. It was a kind of urban "scorched earth" warfare, similar to the way the Russians had resisted Napoleon's capture of Moscow by burning their capital. Some of the fires were due to direct hits by Versailles shells. But the Communards did set many buildings on fire for purposes of tactical withdrawal, or to destroy the symbols of the past. "Burner" Brunel, when evacuating the Ministry of Marine on Tuesday night, 23 May, began to carry out the Commune's order to burn down all hostile houses. He left the rue Royale ablaze, which effectively halted the Versailles advance. Bergeret set fire to the Tuileries Palace as a symbolic act of revenge. He watched the amazing spectacle and scribbled a note, "The last vestiges of Royalty have just vanished."

By Wednesday night, fires were blazing in part of the Palais-Royale, the Palais de Justice, the Préfecture of Police, part of the Louvre and the Council of State. The surrounding streets were also on fire. The next

overleaf: Paris ablaze

day, Thursday, the historic medieval Hôtel de Ville was on fire, although Delescluze had wanted to remain there defending it to the end. Notre Dame just escaped being set alight by the National Guard who were warned of the danger to the wounded in the nearby hospital. The dry, hot weather and the fires made Paris seem like an inferno. De Goncourt wrote in his Journal on 24 May, "Burning Paris makes this seem like the day of an eclipse . . . All around, like black rain, little pieces of charred paper fall from the sky. The accounts and records of France."

In this atmosphere the scare story of the incendiaries (*pétroleuses*) spread like the fires. It seems to have been the Versailles newspapers that first wrote about these

Hôtel de Ville in flames

bands of women. "These furies . . . armed with cans containing a mixture of petrol, tallow and sulphur, slip into houses and, after lighting a fire, escape." The stories were widely believed and many women were denounced and executed in the street. So great did the fear become that householders bricked up their cellar windows, and kept all the ground floor windows shut for weeks during that hot summer.

Execution of suspected pétroleuse

Most of the foreign correspondents did not believe the truth of the stories about the *pétroleuses*. Even the Councils of War, set up to try the Communards, were unable to conclusively convict any Communard women of this particular crime. The whole panic appears to have been a case of mass hysteria, with anti-feminist elements in it, like the witch hunts in sixteenth and seventeenth century Europe and America.

So the last hours of the Commune drew near. The

Communards were now fighting from street to street in an ever decreasing space. They were being hemmed in. All attempts to get negotiations going were fruitless. Washburne, the American Minister in Paris, refused to intervene: "All who belong to the Commune and those that sympathize with them will be shot."

Delescluze, weary and ill, asked to be relieved of his office as Delegate for War. That Thursday evening he wrote a farewell letter to his sister. Then, unarmed, with only a cane, he left his companions to walk alone towards the undefended barricade in the Place du Château d'Eau. For a moment the tall old revolutionary was silhouetted against the evening sun. Then he pitched forward as the bullets hit him.

On Friday 26 May it rained. The atmosphere was murky with smoke lying low over the city. The Bastille barricades fell that day with 100 bodies around and behind them. Only the working class district of Belleville remained in Communard hands defended by 1,000 local National Guards. One group of Guards hysterically shot some hostages to bring the total number of hostages killed to 63.

On Saturday evening the last macabre fight took place at the Père-Lachaise cemetery. It was defended by about 200 Communards who were short of ammunition. Hand-to-hand fighting over the graves went on until there was no-one left to fight. The last Communard was killed near Balzac's tomb. The next morning the Versailles troops found the corpse of the Archbishop. In revenge they took 147 Communard prisoners, lined them against the wall of the cemetery and shot them down. That wall at Père-Lachaise is now a place of pilgrimage for the French working people.

By 28 May, the Versailles army controlled and occupied the city. There remained some mopping-up operations to carry out against isolated Communards, who fought until they were killed or until their ammunition ran out.

At midday, one man was defending the barricade in the rue Ramponneau. He continued to hold his position for a quarter of an hour. He fired his last shot, and then walked calmly away.

Later that afternoon Marshal MacMahon published his order to the inhabitants of Paris:

> The French Army has come to your rescue.
> Paris has been delivered.
> At four o'clock our soldiers took the last rebel position.
> At last the fighting is over; order, work and security will reign once more.

The End of the Commune

10

It should have stopped there but it did not. The fighting was over, but not the killing. "Law and order", Versailles variety, was being restored. The cost for the Parisians was terrible. The blackened city with burnt-out buildings and torn up streets, corpses, blood, shell shot and the débris of the fighting everywhere, was now under military law and subject to army patrols who had orders to shoot on sight. De Goncourt wrote on Monday, 29 May, "The clocks no longer strike in the silence of a desert." A day later he noted, "from time to time frightening noises; fusillades and collapsing houses."

Executions took place day and night, as though revenge could not wait a minute longer for satisfaction. People were picked up in the street on the word of an informer, or on the slightest suspicion that they had been barricade fighters. At La Roquette prison 1,900 people were shot in two days. At Mazas prison another 400 were executed without trial. If a suspect was not immediately shot, then he or she was sent to Versailles for examination and trial. Once they had marched there the weary, fearful prisoners were paraded in front of jeering, cursing crowds before reaching the overcrowded stench of the temporary prisons, or when these were full, being crammed into old convict ships.

The devastated streets of Paris

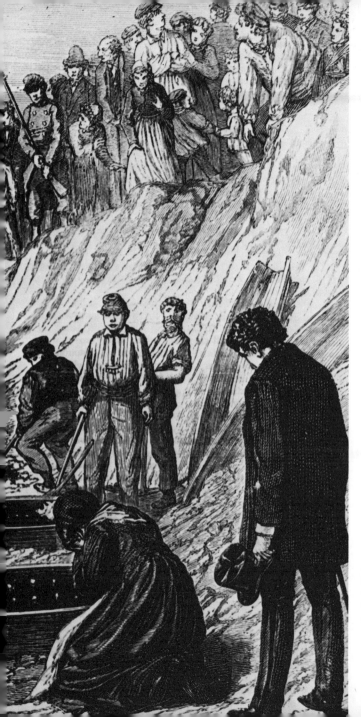

As Paris fell, the death toll rose, and the many dead were hastily buried in mass graves

In Paris hundreds of dead bodies – usually barefoot – lay in the streets or piled up at the central collecting points. Thiers sent a telegram to the provinces: "The ground is paved with their corpses; this terrible spectacle will be a lesson to them." Soon the bodies began to smell and swell, swarms of flies covered them. There was a danger of plague. Since the death carts were too few, every other sort of transport was pressed into service to carry the dead to hastily dug mass graves; or when these were full, to the great funeral pyre burning in eastern Paris. Even the river Seine was streaked with blood. Three hundred bodies in the Buttes-Chaumont lakes swelled with water and floated to the top. The records of Paris show that the city paid for the burial or disposal of 17,000 corpses.

The military authorities were in charge of the trials, known as Councils of War. There were 34,722 Communard prisoners so it is easy to see why the trials lasted from August 1871 to January 1873. The majority of those tried were from the working classes. Only 16 per cent were classified by the army as being from better-off backgrounds. By the end 270, including 8 women, were sentenced to death; 410, with 9 women, to hard labour; and 7,416 including 36 women – Louise Michel among them – to transportation, mainly to New Caledonia near Australia.

It has been estimated that between 20,000 to 25,000 Parisians were killed in the fighting or in the executions without trial afterwards. This is more than the total number killed during the siege or during the two years of Terror, 1793–4, in the great revolution. It is prob-

The trials of those implicated in the Commune lasted six months

able that at least 100,000 Parisians died or disappeared through imprisonment or exile. As a result Paris was deprived of a quarter of her skilled male working population – cabinet makers, tailors, cobblers and many others. The misery and poverty of the remaining families was all that was left behind.

In contrast the losses of the Versailles forces from 2 April amounted to 877 killed, 6,454 wounded plus 63 hostages shot.

The majority of the Communards who managed to escape went into exile in Belgium, England or Switzerland. Those with skills often managed to start businesses or find suitable work if they could learn or speak the language. But they suffered from homesickness and the police restrictions common to political refugees. The less skilled were not so lucky or well prepared, and usually lived in poverty.

Meanwhile wily old Thiers celebrated his victory with a review of the army and a great dinner for the generals. He was made President of the Third Republic in August 1871, but was voted out of that office two years later. The National Assembly had never liked or trusted him.

The National Assembly itself accepted the fact of the republic with some reluctance. It refused to grant an amnesty or free pardon to the Communards until 1880. It tried to purify France of the Commune influence by restoring Church influence over education and morals, strengthening the police and controlling the opposition press. To atone for the so-called "Crimes of the Commune" it built the great white church of Sacré Coeur in Montmartre, and rebuilt the Vendôme Column and the Hôtel de Ville in their original styles. Not until 1879 did the Assembly pluck up courage to return to Paris.

Paris recovered only slowly from the defeat and the repression. In May 1880 Parisians made a great pilgrimage with wreaths to the Père-Lachaise cemetery to commemorate the Communards who had died there. And a month later Trinquet, a cobbler and a brave Communard, was elected to the local council. There was not a hope of another Commune, but at least former Communards could begin to work through the different socialist political parties and put forward some of their ideas.

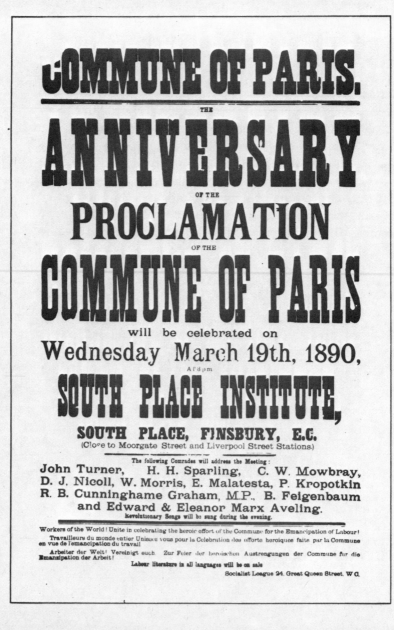

COMMUNE OF PARIS.

THE

ANNIVERSARY

OF THE

PROCLAMATION

OF THE

COMMUNE OF PARIS

will be celebrated on

Wednesday March 19th, 1890,

At 8 p m

SOUTH PLACE INSTITUTE,

SOUTH PLACE, FINSBURY, E.C.

(Close to Moorgate Street and Liverpool Street Stations.)

The following Comrades will address the Meeting :

John Turner, H. H. Sparling, C. W. Mowbray, D. J. Nicoll, W. Morris, E. Malatesta, P. Kropotkin R. B. Cunninghame Graham, M.P., B. Feigenbaum and Edward & Eleanor Marx Aveling.

Revolutionary Songs will be sung during the evening.

Workers of the World ! Unite in celebrating the heroic effort of the Commune for the Emancipation of Labour !

Travailleurs du monde entier Unissez vous pour la Celebration des efforts heroiques faits par la Commune en vue de l'emancipation du travail

Arbeiter der Welt ! Vereinigt euch. Zur Feier der heroischen Austrengungen der Commune für die Emancipation der Arbeit !

Labour literature in all languages will be on sale

Socialist League 24. Great Queen Street. W C.

"Storming Heaven"? 11

The Commune touched the raw nerves of the nineteenth century. There had been other socialist upheavals. But none of them had combined the elements of a workers' government in power with such passionate ideals which reached out beyond the local to the universal human condition. People were also shaken by the cruelty and slaughter of the civil war in France.

Those against the Commune in France and other countries feared that the rise of democracy and of the working class majority would lead to the breakdown of the existing social and economic institutions, and the loss of power. Listen to the Reverend Francis Kilvert, an English clergyman far removed from the scene, as one example of the emotional reaction. He wrote in his diary for 20 March 1871:

> Miserable news from Paris. Another Revolution, barricades, the troops of the line fraternizing with the insurgent National Guard, two Generals shot, two more in the hands and tender mercies of the beastly cowardly Paris mob. These Parisians are the scum of the earth, and Paris is the crater of the volcano, France, and a bottomless pit of revolution and anarchy.

M. François Guizot, the eminent ex-Minister to King Louis Philippe, writing to the London *Times* on

10 April said:

> And now Paris has met with her own disaster. The glory of the siege is followed by the disgrace of falling under the domination of a violent and incapable mob, and becoming prey to a detestable and absurd outbreak of demogogic fury.

The supporters of the Commune at the time had less chance to express their sympathy. Working people and the trades unions were not yet organized to reach across national frontiers, and certainly not rich enough to have their own press. In Europe they all sent messages of support to the Commune – even some from Germany – and organized public meetings where possible. One of the largest demonstrations was held in Hyde Park, London on 16 April, attended by 30,000 people. The case for the Commune was brilliantly defended by Karl Marx in his *Address . . . on the Civil War in France*, published two days after its defeat. Marx realized the originality of the Commune and the importance of its example to the struggles of the industrial workers. It was he too who wrote movingly in a private letter of "these Parisians storming heaven".

The Paris Commune of 1871 was unique. There has never been anything quite like it since. Its manifesto proclaimed that it was "the end of the old world". But that old world temporarily defeated it. Of course in practical terms the Commune could not have survived cut off from the rest of France. But the fact that it existed for 72 days in the midst of a civil war, showed the rest of the world that working people, men and women, the despised and ignored classes, could cooperate and govern themselves. That was a shock and a threat.

The Commune had no time to complete what it wanted to do. It made many mistakes. But its example and humane ideals have moved and inspired people in different ways down to the present day. Lenin studied the successes and failures of the Commune and applied them to the 1917 October Revolution in Russia, taking care that there would be a party dictatorship to lead the people. The Commune was not itself a dictatorship. The Russian anarchists, led by Bakunin, admired it precisely because it rejected the State and listened to the people. During the upheavals in France in May 1968 the ideas of the Commune and its neighbourhood groups were discussed by workers and students in the streets of Paris once again. They faded away as the French government regained control.

The Commune has been described as "a tiger leap" forward in history. Once it had happened, it changed the political possibilities of human beings and could not be ignored. The painter, Renoir, said the Communards were "madmen; but they had in them that little flame which never dies." They were the poets of politics who set alight the ideals of human beings. They could be killed but not suppressed. The battle for the Commune was lost, but the war for its ideals still goes on.

Reading List

The Civil War in France, Karl Marx. First published 1871 (reprinted London 1933)

The Franco-Prussian War and the Commune in Caricature, Susan Lambert. Victoria and Albert Museum 1971

The Fall of Paris: The Siege and Commune, 1870-71, Alistair Horne. Macmillan 1965

History of the Commune of 1871, Prosper-Olivier Lissagaray. First published 1876 (reprinted New York 1969)

Journal, Edmond and Jules de Goncourt. Paris 1887

The Paris Commune, Stewart Edwards. Eyre & Spottiswoode 1971

The Paris Commune, Edward S. Mason. Macmillan, New York 1930

The Paris Commune of 1871, Frank Jellinek. Victor Gollancz 1937 (reprinted 1965)

The Paris Commune of 1871, Eugene Schulkind. Historical Association 1971

The Paris Commune of 1871 – The View from the Left, Eugene Schulkind. London 1972

Paris Libre, J. Rougerie. Paris 1871

The Terrible Year, Alistair Horne. Macmillan 1972

The Women Incendiaries, Edith Thomas. Secker and Warburg 1967

Illustration Sources   *The publishers would like to thank the following for their help with illustrations:*

Messrs. Bulloz: 39
Miss E. Child: 29, 32
Mary Evans Picture Library: 12, 27, 28, 40, 42, 62, 70, 88, 90/91, 96
Patrick Guilbert: 8, 20, 33, 35, 68, 74/75, 77, 83, 101
R. Lalance: 14/15
Macmillan: 24, 29, 30, 36, 38, 54, 60, 64, 82
Marx Memorial Library: 104
Radio Times Hilton Picture Library: 11, 17, 18, 19, 20, 22, 42, 43, 44 46, 50, 52, 53, 56, 62, 76, 78, 79 (top and bottom), 84, 87, 92, 93, 98/99, 101
University of Sussex: 59, 103
Philip Whitfield: 30
Brian and Constance Dear: *map* 16
Jonathan Field: *cover illustration*
and Richard Garnett for his interest and advice.

Word List

ANARCHIST A person who believes in a society without government or force.

BOURGEOISIE Middle class. In socialist theory it is the class opposed to the proletariat or wage-earning class. Many of the bourgeoisie of Paris fled to Versailles when the Commune was declared.

CAPITALIST A person who believes in a social system in which property and the means of production are privately owned.

COMMUNARD A member or supporter of the Commune.

COMMUNE The traditional form of local government in France. It still exists today. The Paris Commune of 1871 was, in fact, the government of the city of Paris, but also claimed to be the forerunner of a new democratic and socialist order for the whole of France.

COMMUNIST A person who believes in a social system in which property and the means of production are owned by the community as a whole. In modern practice usually means a state organized under the sole leadership of the Communist Party, claiming to represent the workers.

DEMOCRACY A form of government which represents the will of the people as directly as possible.

NATIONAL ASSEMBLY The French Parliament. The National Assembly was based in Versailles throughout the period of the Commune.

NATIONAL GUARD An armed citizen militia established in France in 1789 and existing intermittently until 1871. During the Commune it played an important part in the defence of Paris.

PETROLEUSE	Woman incendiary. Many women were rounded up and accused of setting fire to buildings in Paris at the end of the Commune, but there is little evidence that they were guilty of the crime. The term also applied to children.
PROLETARIAT	The class of society that owns no property and is dependent for its livelihood on the sale of its labour.
PROPAGANDA	Information, frequently in the form of posters and newspapers, deliberately designed to advertise the views and opinions of a particular group—often a political one—or to distort and discredit the views of opponents.
RADICAL	A person who believes in fundamental and drastic change.
RED FLAG	The international symbol of socialism. There was a red flag flying on the roof of the Hôtel de Ville in Paris when the Commune was declared.
REPUBLIC	A state in which supreme power rests with the government elected by those citizens entitled to vote. A country without a monarch—as France was when the Emperor Napoleon III abdicated and Thiers formed a government.
REVOLUTIONARY	A person who plans or takes part in the complete overthrow of an established government or political system.
SOCIALIST	A general term for a person who believes that property, capital, and the means of production should belong to the community as a whole.
WORKERS' CO-OPERATIVES	Factories or businesses which are jointly owned and run by the workers who are employed in them. The Commune gave financial assistance to 43 such co-operatives.

Index